Snowy the Barn Owl

Jane Burton

Random House 🏠 New York

Note to parents: Some species of owl are protected by law, and it is illegal in many states to keep any wildlife in captivity. If you or your child should come upon an abandoned or injured owl, *do not touch it*. Notify your game warden or local wildlife management agency so that the animal can be taken to the proper shelter for care.

With thanks to Julie and Gary Huggins for their help

Text and photographs copyright © 1989 by Jane Burton. Copyright © 1989 by Belitha Press. All rights reserved under International and Pan-American Copyright Conventions. Published in the United States by Random House, Inc., New York.

Library of Congress Cataloging-in-Publication Data:
Burton, Jane. Snowy the barn owl. (How animals grow!) SUMMARY: Depicts a barn owl feeding, growing, and learning to hunt and fly during the first year of its life.   ISBN: 0-394-82268-4 (pbk.); 0-394-92268-9 (lib. bdg.)   1. Barn owl—Development—Juvenile literature. 2. Barn owl—Growth—Juvenile literature. [1. Barn owl. 2. Owls. 3. Animals—Infancy] I. Title. II. Series: Burton, Jane. How animals grow!   QL696.S85B87   1989   599'.97   89-42694

Manufactured in Hong Kong   1 2 3 4 5 6 7 8 9 0

Wild barn owls are nesting in an old barn. The mother sits on their eggs, and the father brings mice for her to eat.

The owls have eight eggs. If all eight babies hatch, the owls would not be able to catch enough mice to feed them. So four of the eggs are chosen and put in a warm box called an "incubator." Snowy, the first of them, is already hatching. She has made a hole in the shell with her beak.

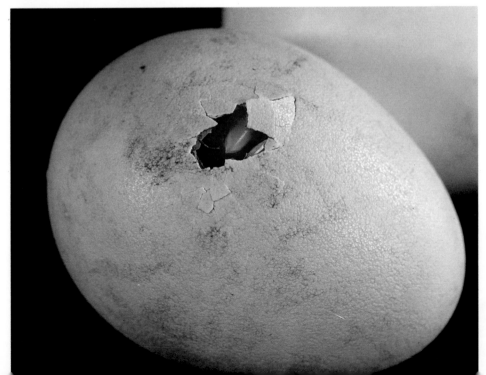

Snowy takes a long time to hatch. It is two days since she made that first hole. Now she is quickly making more holes. She turns inside the egg, so that the small holes connect to make one big crack. Soon the crack is wide enough for Snowy's wing to poke out.

Now the eggshell is held together by only a small piece of shell. Snowy pushes and pushes. Suddenly the two halves burst apart. Snowy kicks and scrambles free.

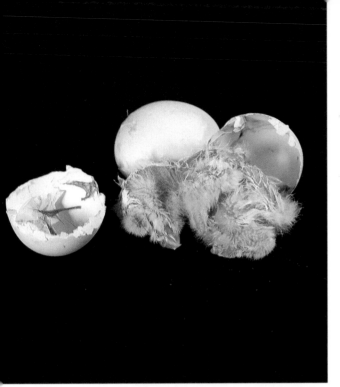

A newborn baby barn owl is not like a baby chick or duckling. It is pink and blind and helpless. A chick or duckling is fluffy and can stand up and walk soon after hatching. Its eyes are wide open. But it will be days before Snowy can even sit up, and weeks before she can see.

Barn owl eggs do not all hatch at the same time. Snowy is two days old when Puff hatches. They sleep curled up together. Polly hatches five days after Puff, and Humpty hatches three days later.

Five days old

Snowy and her sisters stay in their warm bed and are taken out only to be weighed. They are fed regularly four times a day. When Snowy is hungry, she twitters. She is fed in a margarine tub, her head propped over the rim.

Snowy pecks tiny pieces of soft meat from a pair of tweezers. She cannot see the food. But as soon as she feels the tip of the tweezers touch her beak, she opens her mouth. The tweezers are just like a mother barn owl's beak, feeding Snowy.

At first Snowy eats only a tiny amount, but as she eats, she grows. The bigger she grows, the more she can eat. Snowy is weighed each day to make sure she is eating enough.

Eight days old

Snowy is so big already that only her head would fit inside an egg now. She can sit up. She yawns a huge yawn, then settles down to sleep again. Sometimes she sleeps on her belly. Sometimes she goes to sleep on her back with her feet in the air. She twitters in her sleep, and her wings twitch. She must be dreaming that she is flying!

Twelve days old

When Snowy wants to shift to a warmer spot, she shuffles along on her bottom. Or she can half-stand and stumble around, like a little old man. She feels the way with her beak.

Fifteen days old

Snowy's eyes are opening at last. She sits in her feeding tub after a huge meal. Her belly is as round and tight as a tennis ball. Alarming belly rumbles are heard. She shakes and shivers so that the whole tub vibrates. She must go back into her warm bed to digest her meal.

Snowy and her three sisters live in a nursery cage now, heated by an electric lamp. They crowd together under the lamp to warm up after dinner. Their first feathers, called "down," are not enough to keep them warm yet.

Sixteen days old

Three in a boat and one overboard! Puff and Polly and Snowy can just fit in the tub, but there's no room for Humpty. All the owlets are hungry again and crying for food. They search around with their beaks. When Snowy and Humpty touch beaks, each one thinks that the other is going to feed her. They jab and bite beaks until Humpty topples backward.

After they eat, it is weighing time again. Snowy tests a weight with her beak.

Twenty-six days old

Snowy has sprouted a second coat of down.
Now that she is all fluffy and white, she *almost*
looks pretty. At mealtimes there is only room in
the tub for the two smallest owls, who are still
just eating tiny bits of meat. Snowy is so big
that she can eat a whole mouse in one gulp,
but she has trouble swallowing its tail. She looks
a little uncomfortable, but such a big meal
keeps her quiet for a long time.

Thirty days old

The owlets have grown so much that now, when they cluster under the lamp, they hit their heads on it if they're not careful.

Cracker the kitten is exploring the barn owl nursery. She and Snowy are the same age. They look the same size. But the kitten is heavier than Snowy. If only they would sit still for a moment, they could be weighed!

Thirty-two days old

Every day Snowy swallows four mice whole. She digests the meat but not the hard parts. All the mouse bones and fur form a neat package, or "pellet," inside her, which she will spit out.

While Snowy is waiting to spit out a pellet, she looks very sick. Then she just opens her mouth, out pops the pellet, and she is hungry again.

Thirty-eight days old

Light brown feathers have been sprouting all this time underneath Snowy's down. Now her wing feathers are no longer hidden in the fluff. Short feathers around her face form a disk. She is beginning to look more like a barn owl and less like a soft, cuddly toy. She stands sturdily on spread toes. She can run and climb, but she cannot fly yet.

Two months old

All the owlets can help themselves to their food
now. Snowy has lost most of her down, but
Humpty is still covered with it. Puff and Polly
are still downy too. Little tufts of molted white
down drift everywhere.

The four owlets live in the hay barn. They
may still look cute, but they are *not* pets. They
are growing up into dangerous birds of prey.
Soon they will learn to catch mice for themselves.

Three months old

Snowy is very beautiful now that she has lost all her down. But she is fierce, like a wild owl should be.

All four young owls can fly, but not very well yet. They practice a lot so they can strengthen their wing muscles. Snowy whirs her wings and hops up and down without actually taking off.

The owls often squabble over their food. Snowy is clutching a mouse in one foot. She hisses at Polly and spreads her wings to protect her prey.

Six months old

The owls have all flown from the hay barn. They hunt for themselves now. Snowy wings silently over the fields at night, like a huge white moth. She watches and listens for wild mice feeding and scampering in the grass below.

Other barn owls are also around. Boris screeches as he flies. Snowy and Boris meet. They like each other and become a pair.

One year old

Boris and Snowy have a growing family of their own. When the baby owlets are tiny and pink, Snowy sits on them all the time to keep them warm. Boris goes out hunting and brings the food back to Snowy. She pulls off tiny shreds of meat and touches her babies' beaks so that they know to take the food from her. Now that Snowy's owlets are large and downy, she can leave them for a while to help Boris hunt. They will need to bring hundreds of mice to the nest before the owlets are grown up and ready to hunt for themselves.